EDGE OF MED

GENETICS
BREAKTHROUGHS

HEATHER E. SCHWARTZ

MAYO CLINIC PRESS KIDS

To Philip, Jaz, and Griffin

MAYO CLINIC PRESS KIDS | An imprint of Mayo Clinic Press
200 First St. SW
Rochester, MN 55905
mcpress.mayoclinic.org
To stay informed about Mayo Clinic Press, please subscribe to our free e-newsletter at mcpress.mayoclinic.org or follow us on social media.

The medical information in this book is true and complete to the best of our knowledge. This book is intended as an informative guide for those wishing to learn more about health issues. It is not intended to replace, countermand or conflict with advice given to you by your own physician. The ultimate decision concerning your care should be made between you and your doctor. Information in this book is offered with no guarantees. The author and publisher disclaim all liability in connection with the use of this book. The views expressed are the author's personal views, and do not necessarily reflect the policy or position of Mayo Clinic.

For bulk sales to employers, member groups and health-related companies, contact Mayo Clinic at SpecialSalesMayoBooks@mayo.edu.

Proceeds from the sale of every book benefit important medical research and education at Mayo Clinic.

ISBN: 978-1-945564-87-1 (paperback) | 978-1-945564-86-4 (library binding) | 978-1-945564-88-8 (ebook) | 979-8-88770-076-2 (multiuser PDF) | 979-8-88770-075-5 (multiuser ePub)

Library of Congress Control Number: 2022942581
Library of Congress Cataloging-in-Publication Data is available upon request.

TABLE OF CONTENTS

MICROSCOPIC GENES,
GIANT CHANGE

For as long as she could remember, Victoria Gray had been scared to fly on a plane. Gray had sickle cell disease. This caused her body's cells to react to changes in their environment, such as temperature and **altitude**. These changes could cause Gray severe pain. She was terrified to find out what changes might affect her body on a flight.

In 2019, Gray had an experimental **procedure** to help stop the painful reactions her disease caused. Doctors removed cells from Gray's body. They edited, or changed, certain **genes** in the cells. Then they **reinserted** the cells. The edited genes were meant to create **proteins** that blocked Gray's painful symptoms. The procedure worked! By the next year, Gray took her first plane ride without pain.

Scientists began studying genetics more than 150 years ago. This research, along with new technologies, has led to many breakthroughs. Modern gene treatments can build resistance to diseases and treat disease symptoms.

4

Typical red blood cells (*round*) and sickle blood cells (*oblong*). The sickle cells are more rigid and more easily irritated than the typical cells.

THE FATHER OF
GENETICS

In the mid-1800s, Czech scientist Gregor Mendel wanted to know more about how human **traits** are passed down through generations. Mendel thought he could learn by experimenting with plants. He chose pea plants because they came in many varieties and produced **offspring** quickly.

Still, Mendel's experiments were slow work. He spent eight years watching the plants reproduce naturally. He also bred them himself. Mendel observed pod shape, pea color, and other traits. By 1865, he had studied 28,000 pea plants!

Mendel's research led him to develop the principles of **inheritance**. These are the law of **segregation**, the law of independent **assortment**, and the law of **dominance**.

The law of segregation explained how inherited genes are separated, so a child inherits a trait from only one parent. The law of independent assortment explained that genes for different traits are independent. Inheriting one trait does not mean a child will inherit another. The law of dominance said that **dominant genes** override **recessive genes** to produce traits.

Mendel became known as the "father of genetics." Scientists still use his principles to explain how traits are passed along in humans.

Gregor Mendel's findings made a huge impact on science. But they were rejected during his lifetime! Mendel's principles of inheritance weren't accepted until many decades after his death.

DISCOVERING
DNA

In 1869, Swiss scientist Johann Friedrich Miescher studied white blood cells. It was a tough and dirty job. Miescher collected patients' used bandages from a nearby hospital. First, he washed any **pus** off the bandages. Then he experimented on the dried blood.

Miescher separated different parts of the white blood cells in order to identify them. While separating one day, he made a discovery. Miescher identified an unknown **molecule** from the nucleus. He called this molecule *nuclein*.

The modern term for nuclein is deoxyribonucleic acid (DNA). Miescher had discovered the substance that carries genetic information inside cells! It was a huge step forward in studying genes and **heredity**.

Scientists furthered Miescher's research in the following decades. The study of DNA affected the medical field in many positive ways. It allowed doctors to learn whether people are at risk for disease, create medications, and much more!

DNA consists of two spiraling strands joined by four chemical bases. These bases are adenine, cytosine, guanine, and thymine. The bases pair and create rungs. Their order creates genes.

DISCOVERING
CHROMOSOMES

Ten years after Miescher first identified DNA, a scientist in Germany made another genetic discovery. Technology in 1879 made viewing cells through a **microscope** difficult. Scientists could get a better look at cells by staining parts of them using dyes. This is how Walther Flemming discovered a material within the nucleus of a cell. Flemming called this material *chromatin.*

Later scientists would rename Flemming's discovery *chromosomes.* Chromosomes are long strands of DNA, tightly coiled together. Chromosomes allow genetic information to be copied during cell division. DNA carries information that tells the cells how to function.

Other scientists built on Flemming's work. They learned that each species has a certain number of chromosomes. German scientist Theodor Boveri studied roundworms and sea urchin eggs. US scientist Walter Sutton also studied sea creatures. In early 1900, both scientists used Mendel's principles to learn how chromosomes pass from parents to offspring.

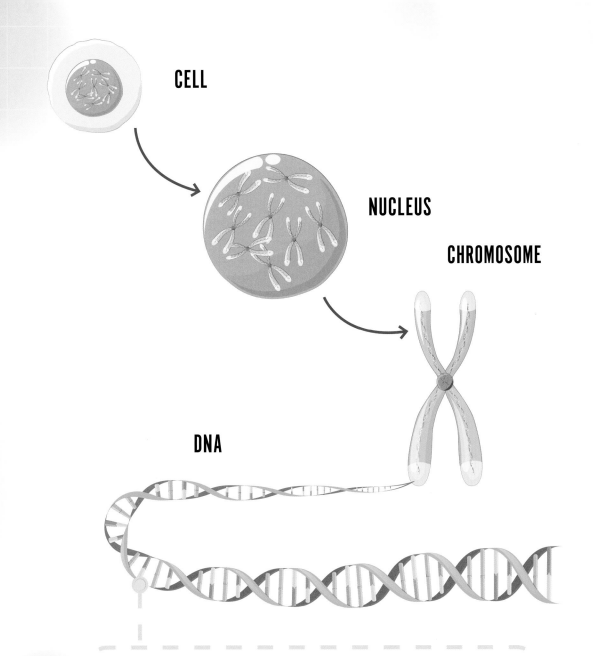

CELL

NUCLEUS

CHROMOSOME

DNA

Every human cell has a center, called a nucleus. Each nucleus holds 46 chromosomes. Chromosomes are made up of coiled strands of DNA. Sections of DNA make up genes. Each chromosome can hold thousands of genes!

LINKING
GENES AND DISEASE

In the early 1900s, English doctor Sir Archibald Garrod studied people with a rare, inherited disease. Alkaptonuria causes a certain acid to build up in the body. The acid changes the color of **urine**. The disease is also called black urine disease.

Garrod gathered information on families living with alkaptonuria. Then he followed Mendel's principles of inheritance to study their traits. Garrod concluded a recessive gene caused the disease. A person only got the disease if both of their parents had this gene and passed it on with the mutation that causes the disease.

Genes act like **templates** for making proteins in the body. One type of protein they make is enzymes. Garrod formed a **theory** about the recessive gene he studied. He felt it was **defective**, creating an enzyme that didn't work right. This enzyme caused alkaptonuria.

Garrod's theory was proven true. And it explained other diseases too. This made waves in the medical world. Before then, people had not known that human diseases could be inherited!

Typical urine crystals (*top*) and dark urine crystals (*bottom right*) of a person with alkaptonuria

Alkaptonuria can darken certain parts of the body, such as earlobes and spots in the eye.

GENE AND CHROMOSOME KEY

By 1910, Mendel had created the principles of inheritance. Flemming had discovered chromosomes. Then US scientist Thomas Hunt Morgan broke new ground that year.

Morgan studied fruit flies, which typically have red eyes. But one male fly in his lab had white eyes. Morgan bred this fly with a red-eyed fly. Both the male and female babies were born with red eyes. Morgan decided the gene for white eyes must be recessive. Then he bred the offspring together. Some were born with white eyes! Morgan realized all the white-eyed flies were male.

From his experiments, Morgan concluded that some traits are linked to a being's sex. Scientists knew a certain chromosome **determined** sex. So, Morgan decided some genes may only be on certain chromosomes! This was a key to unlocking future genetics research.

Thomas Hunt Morgan performed his fruit fly experiments in the "fly room" at Columbia University in New York. The room's shelves held many glass jars containing the flies being studied.

CHERISSE A. MARCOU, PHD

MAYO CLINIC

Q: When did you first become interested in genetics?

A: My interest in genetics first began in 2003 when the Human Genome Project was completed. It is one of the world's greatest scientific accomplishments and was the starting point to the rapid advancements in human biology.

Q: What is the most exciting thing happening in genetics research?

A: Well, there is never only a single exciting thing happening in the field of genomics. But a recent accomplishment that will continue to advance our

understanding of the human genome is revealing the first truly complete human genome sequence in 2022. This project filled in the remaining gaps of DNA sequence from the first project in 2003.

Q: How can genetics research help treat and cure rare diseases?

A: Genomics research has uncovered the molecular causes of many different rare diseases, bringing an understanding of the biological basis of disease and driving better treatment and management for patients. It is estimated that approximately 80 percent of rare diseases have a genetic component. But because these diseases are rare, many patients spend years going to different medical specialists before they finally get the correct diagnosis. This highlights the importance of comprehensive genomics approaches in uncovering the underlying causes and providing new ways for tailored disease management and ending the rare disease "diagnostic odyssey" for families. Identifying a molecular diagnosis is a key step that benefits the patients and their families.

Q: What is the most rewarding part of working in medicine for you?

A: Four words—The patients we serve! Each and every day I am inspired to continue my work in laboratory medicine and pathology to contribute to the promise of precision medicine. I am humbled and honored to have a role in solving medical mysteries and unlocking the future of health care **delivery**.

EXTRA CHROMOSOME
KICKS OFF NEW FIELD

French doctor Jérôme Lejeune treated children. In 1958, he took a special interest in researching children with Down syndrome. Lejeune wanted to understand what made these children **unique**.

Lejeune studied the traits and genetics of children with Down syndrome. He was studying one child's chromosomes when he made a discovery. There was a good reason the child, and others with Down syndrome, were unique. Most people have 46 chromosomes. But people with Down syndrome have 47 chromosomes.

Lejeune concluded an extra chromosome was the genetic cause of Down syndrome. He also found that having the extra chromosome was not hereditary. This discovery inspired research in a new field of genetics! Cytogenetics blends the study of cell biology with the study of genes.

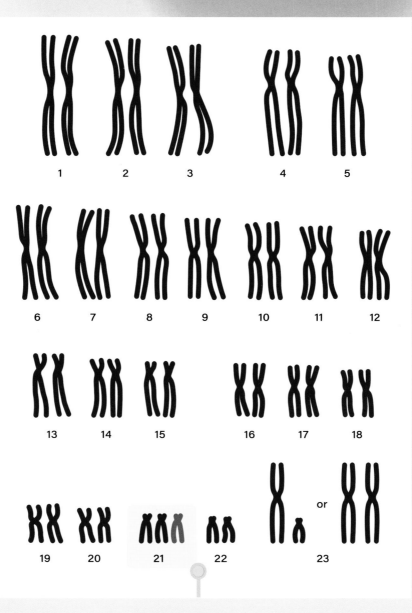

Having an extra chromosome is called trisomy. Down syndrome is also referred to as trisomy 21 because of the presence of a third copy of chromosome 21.

GENE MAPPING
DISEASE

In the 1970s, US doctor Nancy Wexler began a study on Huntington's disease. The inherited disease can't be cured and causes early death. In 1979, Wexler traveled to Venezuela, where a family had the world's highest rate of Huntington's disease. Wexler's study included more than 18,000 people from the extended family!

Wexler gathered more than 4,000 blood samples from the family. She studied their DNA to learn how the disease passed between generations. This work took years. In 1983, Wexler and a team of researchers discovered a genetic marker for Huntington's disease on a chromosome. This marker told them which chromosome held the gene causing the disease. It was the first time scientists had mapped the location of a gene that causes disease.

It took Wexler and her team another ten years to identify the causal gene. This is because a chromosome can contain thousands of genes. In 1993, Wexler's team found the gene that causes

Huntington's disease. This allowed doctors to create a blood test to detect the gene in people at risk from inheriting the disease. If the test comes back positive, people know there's a chance they could pass the gene to their offspring. This helps them make knowledgeable decisions in shaping their family.

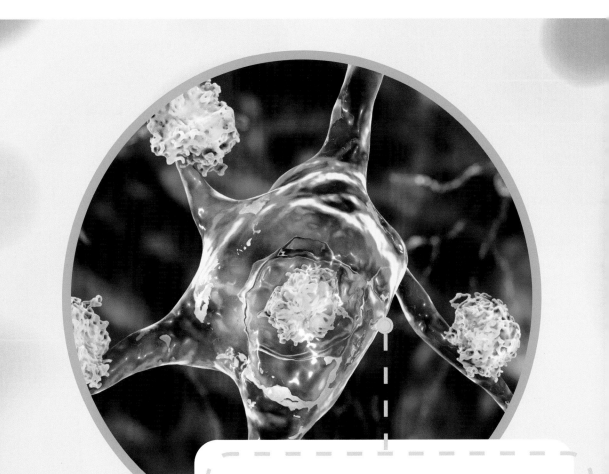

The gene that causes Huntington's disease is called HTT. The protein made by this gene causes nerve cells in the brain to break down (*pictured*).

GENE TREATMENT
SAVES CHILD

When Ashanti de Silva was born in 1985, she inherited a severe **immunodeficiency** disease (SCID). Her body couldn't fight **infections**. By age four, Ashanti was dying.

Doctors knew two broken copies of a gene were behind Ashanti's SCID. They hoped an experimental gene treatment could cure her. Research had proven new genes could be inserted into plants and animals. What if this practice could help improve a human's **immune system**?

In 1990, doctors removed some of Ashanti's blood. They inserted working copies of the broken gene into her blood cells. Then, they reinserted the blood cells back into Ashanti. It was the first gene therapy performed on a **pediatric** patient.

The gene therapy did not cure Ashanti's SCID. But she grew healthier! The new, working genes helped her immune system fight infection. Ashanti lived into adulthood. And her case led researchers to further study gene therapy. They hoped it could improve, or even cure, other genetic diseases.

Like Ashanti de Silva, David Vetter (*right*) had severe immunodeficiency disease (SCID). David died in 1984, the year before Ashanti was born. He was 12 years old. David lived his short life in a sterile bubble to prevent him from being exposed to germs and getting infections.

GENE EDITING
SOLVES PAIN

When Victoria Gray was three months old in 1985, she was diagnosed with sickle cell disease. The disease caused attacks of severe pain.

In 2012, French scientist Emmanuelle Charpentier and US scientist Jennifer Doudna together developed a gene editing technology called CRISPR. In 2013, five teams of scientists first used CRISPR on human and animal cells. In 2019, when Gray was 34, she signed up to be the first person treated with CRISPR.

CRISPR delivered an enzyme and **ribonucleic acid** into a cell. This allowed the cell's chromosome to be cut in a certain spot to add or remove certain genes. Doctors had used gene editing before. But CRISPR made it faster, easier, less expensive, and more exact.

Doctors removed billions of cells from Gray's body. They used CRISPR to edit the cells so they would produce a protein to stop her pain. Then, they reinserted the cells into Gray.

Jennifer Doudna (*left*) and Emmanuelle Charpentier hold a model of a CRISPR enzyme in 2017.

Within months, Gray's life changed. The painful attacks stopped! Doctors learned CRISPR gene editing could help millions of people around the world living with sickle cell disease.

NEW HOPE FOR
STOPPING COVID-19

The **COVID-19 pandemic** changed life worldwide for many years, starting in 2020. The coronavirus causing COVID-19 affected people differently. Some people grew very ill and died. Others had only mild symptoms. Scientists wanted to learn why. And they thought genes might be the answer.

Researchers at Minnesota's Mayo Clinic looked for clues. They studied DNA from 71,000 people. In 2022, they learned some people have genes that increase certain proteins in their body. These proteins made them more **susceptible** to symptoms from disease. Others have genes that decrease those proteins and give protection from disease.

Mayo scientists continued to study their findings. They wanted to use the information about genes to help future patients. COVID-19 killed more than 6.3 million people worldwide between 2020 and 2022. Researchers hope gene editing or gene therapy could prevent or treat the disease, saving millions of lives in the future.

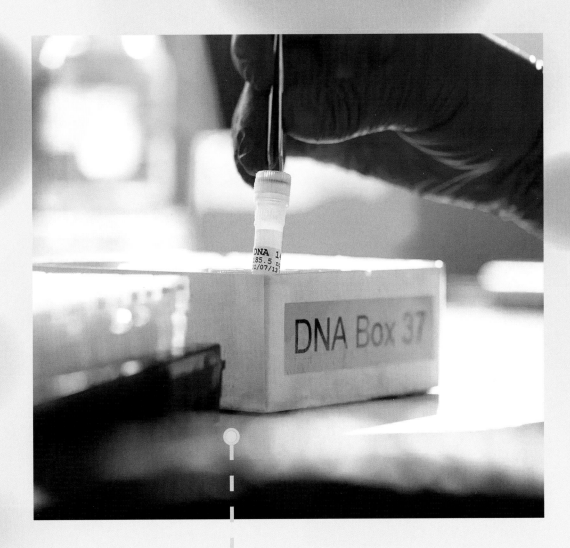

ACE2 and *TMPRESS2* were the two proteins the Mayo team identified in its COVID-19 DNA study. These proteins provide entry points for the virus causing COVID-19 to invade cells.

TIMELINE

1869

Friedrich Miescher discovers DNA.

EARLY 1900s

Sir Archibald Garrod discovers a link between genes and inherited diseases.

1865

Gregor Mendel establishes the principles of inheritance, which modern doctors and scientists still use today.

1910

Thomas Hunt Morgan proves chromosomes carry information that is inherited.

1879

Walther Flemming discovers the chromosome. He theorizes there is a link between chromosomes and heredity.

1990

Ashanti de Silva is the world's first pediatric gene therapy patient.

1958

Jérôme Lejeune learns an extra chromosome causes Down syndrome. His work leads to the field of cytogenetics.

2022

Mayo Clinic researchers reveal a genetic reason why some people develop severe COVID-19.

1983

A team led by Nancy Wexler gene maps Huntington's disease, proving it is passed from parent to child by a gene.

2012

Emmanuelle Charpentier and Jennifer Doudna develop CRISPR, a gene editing technology. It can change how genes work to help people with diseases.

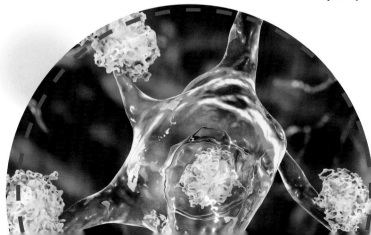

GLOSSARY

altitude—the height above the ground or above the sea level

assortment—a collection of different sorts of things

COVID-19 pandemic—a global spread of the SARS-COV2 virus beginning in early 2020

defective—having a flaw or error

deliver—to send or bring. This action is called delivery.

determine—to decide firmly

dominance—the state or condition of being more powerful or stronger than something else

dominant gene—a gene that is stronger than the matching gene in another strand of DNA.

gene—the smallest unit of characteristics passed from parent to offspring. The study of genes is called genetics. Things relating to genes are genetic.

heredity—the natural process by which traits are passed from a parent to a child. A passed trait is described as hereditary.

immune system—the body's system that fights off disease and infection

immunodeficiency—the inability of the body to fight infections and other diseases

infection—the entrance and growth of germs in the body

inherit—to receive from a parent. This process is called inheritance.

insert—to place something into another thing. Doing this after removal is to reinsert.

microscope—a device containing a powerful magnifying glass used to see items invisible to the human eye

molecule—the smallest possible amount of a particular substance that has all the characteristics of that substance

offspring—the young of an animal or plant

pediatric—relating to the branch of medicine that cares for infants and children

procedure—a certain course of action or steps taken to achieve a result

protein—a molecule of amino acids that is essential to body function

pus—thick, yellowy liquid that forms at an infection

recessive gene—a gene that is less strong than the matching gene in another strand of DNA

ribonucleic acid—a copy of DNA that is typically single stranded

segregation—the practice of separating according to groups or type

susceptible—being very likely to be affected by something

template—a pattern used as a guide

theory—a group of ideas meant to explain something

trait—a quality that makes one person or thing different from another

unique—unlike anything else

LEARN MORE

Britannica Kids: Genetics
https://kids.britannica.com/kids/article/genetics/353170
method/index.htm

How to Be Good at Science, Technology, and Engineering. London: DK Children, 2018.

LaRocca, Rajani. *The Secret Code Inside You: All About Your DNA.* New York: Little Bee Books, 2021.

Mayo Clinic: Science Saturday—The Benefits of Genetic Testing for Healthy People
https://newsnetwork.mayoclinic.org/discussion/science-saturday-the-benefits-of-genetic-testing-for-healthy-people/

INDEX

PHOTO ACKNOWLEDGMENTS

American Philosophical Society/Science Source, p. 15; CHIARI_VFX/iStockphoto, cover (chromosomes); DC Studio/Shutterstock Images, cover (scientist); Designua/Shutterstock Images, p. 11; Dr_Microbe/iStockphoto, pp. 21, 29 (bottom); JuSun/iStockphoto, cover (DNA); Mayo Clinic, pp. 16, 27; Medical Heritage Library, Inc./Flickr, p. 13 (main); Michelle Goebel/Wikimedia Commons, p. 23; Ozgu Arslan/iStockphoto, p. 9; PeopleImages/iStockphoto, cover (child on bike); Rujirat Boonyong/iStockphoto, pp. 19, 29 (top); traffic_analyzer/iStockphoto, cover (background); ttsz/iStockphoto, p. 13 (inset); Victor Josan/Shutterstock Images, back cover, p. 5; Wellcome Collection, pp. 7, 28; Yomiuri Shimbun/AP Images, p. 25